Julian Burnside

On Privilege

Writers in the *On Series*

The discussion of any subject is a right that you have brought into the world with your heart and tongue. Resign your heart's blood before you part with this inestimable privilege of man.

Percy Bysshe Shelley, *An Address to the Irish People*, 1812

hachette
AUSTRALIA

Published in Australia and New Zealand in 2020
by Hachette Australia
(an imprint of Hachette Australia Pty Limited)
Level 17, 207 Kent Street, Sydney NSW 2000
www.hachette.com.au

First published in 2009 by Melbourne University Publishing

10 9 8 7 6 5 4 3 2 1

A catalogue record for this
book is available from the
National Library of Australia

ISBN: 978 0 7336 4401 6 (paperback)

Original cover concept by Nada Backovic Design
Text design by Alice Graphics
Typeset by Typeskill
Printed and bound in Australia by McPherson's Printing Group

The paper this book is printed on is certified against the
Forest Stewardship Council® Standards. McPherson's Printing
Group holds FSC® chain of custody certification SA-COC-005379.
FSC® promotes environmentally responsible, socially beneficial

I saw privilege before I heard the word or learnt its meaning.

My father's parents lived in an enormous house in Toorak. With a vast garden, a covered walk, a pond, a rose garden and a tennis court, it stood as a dignified monument to my grandfather's mercantile success. A millionaire in the days of pounds, when being a millionaire really meant something, he was old, rich, clever, kindly, modest and powerful. My grandparents held splendid parties at which they entertained politicians, industrialists and people who were interesting or glamorous or both. They once had a weekender at Blairgowrie: a bluestone mansion with its own tennis court, nine-hole putting green and private jetty. In that magical world, my father grew up.

As a child, I saw these things but did not question them. I knew that most people did not live in mansions like this—our family home was modest by comparison, but I took for granted the fact that we had a tennis court at home, too. If I had thought about it (which I did not), I would probably have assumed that some people choose to have a tennis court, and others do not. That's how you think as a five-year-old. It would be some years before I realised that my parents and my grandparents enjoyed privileges that many would envy.

My father was a cherished only son. He was also a keen photographer. Photographs he took while he was a medical student preserve, on ghostly glass negatives, images that could have been drawn from the world of Jay Gatsby or the Mitfords: handsome cars, elegant tennis parties and mysterious parlour games. Tightly coiffed women and complacent, shiny young men are preserved as if in aspic.

My father's parents helped make the rules. They got what they wanted, and he got what he wanted. Nothing was too good for him: a first-rate education at

Melbourne Grammar and the University of Melbourne, English suits, a Riley sports car.

But then, the Second World War.

The Japanese prison camp at Changi in Singapore is justly notorious. Thirty per cent of those who were held there did not survive. They died of starvation, disease and mistreatment, of broken bodies and broken hearts. My father was there from February 1942 to October 1945. He survived, but came out changed.

Judging by the tone and content of the diary he kept every day in Changi, he went in as a priggish, spoilt, privileged young plutocrat, for whom wealth, position and success were unstated assumptions. He came out as a genuine egalitarian who believed everyone his equal in humanity and potential. The photographs he took in Changi, until the *Kempetai*[1] cracked down on contraband, show the deteriorating condition of the prisoners and the wretchedness of their circumstances. The photographs he took in the camp immediately after the end of hostilities show most of the survivors reduced to walking skeletons. But he noted at one point in his diary that 'company is more important than circumstances'. He rarely spoke of his time as a prisoner of war. When he did, it was clear that while he would never have chosen to be in Changi, he considered it a privilege to have experienced and survived it.

After the war, as a consultant surgeon at the Alfred Hospital, he was a powerful, authoritative figure, both feared and admired—feared because of his exacting standards in surgery, and admired not because of his family or schooling, but because of his skill and dedication. He had the privileges of wealth, education and talent. He never misused the opportunities they opened up for him. And although his parents' wealth was eventually dissipated by bad luck and bad management, he used his education and his talent to pioneer new methods of surgery and for the good of many thousands of patients. He never, as far as I observed, acted as though privilege entitled him to anything hard work would not earn.

I had not looked up the dictionary definition of *privilege* until I sat down to write this essay. An informed guess turned out to be more or less accurate: *privi-legium* or 'private law'—a special law having reference to an individual—is the Latin origin of the word. Originally, the effect of a *privi-legium* on the individual might be good or bad: it might confer an advantage or benefit, or it might impose a penalty or forfeiture.[2]

Historically one of the most distinctive sources of privilege was the divine right of kings—a hallmark of the Stuart monarchy—whereby the King ruled above the law and could dispense with it entirely in particular cases. This right was put into practice by Charles I, who was running short of money. Parliament would not grant supply, so he asked various nobles to advance compulsory 'loans', with no definite plan for repayment. Sir Thomas Darnel and four others refused to pay, and in response the King ordered their arrest. When they sought habeas corpus, the gaoler answered the suit by saying the five were held '*per speciale mandatum Regis*'.[3]

The question whether the king ruled apart from the law, or was subject to it, was a major source of the discord between the King and the parliament that culminated in the English Civil War. When Charles lost both the war and his head, that particular form of privilege disappeared from English society. Since the Restoration, British monarchs have accepted that they rule subject to the law and cannot set it aside.

It is one of history's ironies that the USA has preserved some aspects of this kind of privilege. Except in cases of impeachment, the US President has the power to grant reprieves and pardons for offences against the USA[4]—a power that bears a passing resemblance to the power of the Stuart kings to dispense with the law in particular cases. But this pales into insignificance when compared with what President George W Bush, aided by a small cadre of lawyers, did in the

immediate aftermath of September 11:
he asserted the right to mount military
attacks on US citizens in the USA, and he
authorised wire-tapping of US citizens in
violation of the Fourth Amendment.[5]

The similarity with the Stuart kings
does not end there. In the wake of
September 11 and the US invasion of
Afghanistan, Bush established a prison
camp at Guantanamo Bay in Cuba with
the intention of placing detainees beyond
the reach of the law, so that the President
alone could determine their fate. From
the outset, the world was told that the
people held at Guantanamo Bay were the
'worst of the worst'; they were 'terrorists
and killers and people who hate freedom'.
In the tunnel vision of George W Bush,

terrorism had sprung, fully formed, into existence on September 11, 2001; it was therefore necessary to find a new way of dealing with a 'new problem'.

As a matter of legal principle, there was no 'new problem'. Combatants captured in Afghanistan during the hostilities were either prisoners of war or they were criminal suspects. Domestic and international laws deal comprehensively with both cases. There is no ground between the two possibilities. The regime for the treatment of prisoners of war is clearly established by the Geneva Convention, to which the USA is a party. Relevantly, it provides for humane treatment, for no interrogation beyond name, rank and serial number, and for release at the end of hostilities unless tried for war crimes. The regime for treatment of criminal suspects is also clear: they must be treated humanely; they are not obliged to answer questions; they may not be held in prolonged detention without charge; they have a prima facie entitlement to bail when charged; and (importantly in these circumstances) criminal charges are generally to be dealt with in the country where the offences occurred. In either case, and in all circumstances, there is an absolute prohibition on the use of torture. This is recognised as a universal norm of international law and is the subject of the Convention against Torture, to which most countries, including the USA and Afghanistan, are parties.

President Obama has announced that the prison at Guantanamo is to be closed. It remains to be seen whether the CIA will continue to operate black sites around the fringe of the civilised world. Even so, the closure of Guantanamo is a welcome end to a time of unaccountable betrayal of fundamental values. Unfortunately, there comes a time in the history of nations when, for some unaccountable reason, basic values and accepted principles are diluted, betrayed or cast aside. The pretext may be external threat, internal strife or any other great force that is thought to call for an extraordinary response.

Faced with very clear legal limits, President Bush acted, in substance, as the Stuart kings had. He acted as if he could set aside the law and implement his own conception of right, and he did this with help from Department of Justice employees. (The process was also driven, and to a significant extent guided, by Dick Cheney's lawyer David Addington, who had long shared Cheney's ideological concern that Congress was too powerful, and the executive branch not powerful enough.) Bush marshalled the department's best and brightest to identify limits to the treatment of detainees held at Guantanamo Bay. They obliged by suggesting ways in which inmates could be held neither as prisoners of war nor as criminal suspects. By a little sleight of hand, of which they were entirely unaware, the prisoners in Guantanamo lost all their rights: not by attainder of blood but by classification as 'enemy combatants'.

In a series of notorious memos prepared in early 2002, Department of Justice lawyers noted that this classification would free US interrogators of the inconvenience of criminal charges if they happened to injure or kill prisoners during interrogation. They also found torture a difficult concept to pin down, suggesting that while the USA would never use torture, it would nevertheless be OK to use stress positions, waterboarding and the other countless cruel indignities later revealed at Abu Ghraib. The White House prefers to call these methods 'coercion'. The rest of the world recognises these techniques as torture. Changing the name does not change the thing. Doubtless the victims were enchanted by these etymological quibbles.

Bush's authorisation of torture at Guantanamo Bay closely mirrors the actions of James I, who on 6 November 1605 personally authorised the torture of John Johnson, otherwise known as Guy Fawkes. It was deeply ironic to see Bush stumble back to the seventeenth century, especially given the close connection between the excesses of the Stuarts and the foundational impulse of the American Republic. In protest against Charles I and his treatment of Sir Thomas Darnel, the parliament presented the Petition of Right in 1627, which later served as the basis for the US Bill of Rights.

But if Bush saw the irony, he was not deterred by it: the establishment of a prison at Guantanamo Bay was intended specifically to put prisoners beyond the protection of the US Bill of Rights. When that device was defeated in the Supreme Court, Congress passed the *Military Commissions Act of 2006*. Despite the central role of the ancient writ of habeas corpus in protecting the rule of law, and notwithstanding its honoured place in the US Constitution, the Act denied prisoners at Guantanamo Bay access to habeas corpus. Thus the detainees were specially exempted from one of the law's most revered and powerful protections. That exemption was finally struck down by the US Supreme Court in June 2008.[6]

But by then, the population of Guantanamo Bay had fallen dramatically. More than half of the original detainees turned out not to be killers or terrorists or the worst of the worst—just the unluckiest of the unlucky. After a year or two or three of coercion and misery, they have been repatriated, without apology, without compensation, without even an explanation. It is not clear whether the US government will try to reclaim the bounty they paid to the Northern Alliance for these prisoners.

The first military commission began in July 2008, six years after the 'privileged' were rounded up and thrown—trussed, gagged and hooded—into the legal black hole of Guantanamo Bay. The first defendant was Salim Ahmed Hamdan. He probably did not realise how privileged he was, etymologically speaking, in being the victim of the special law-breaking efforts of the US President or, more fortunately, in not being one of the suspects who were beaten to death by US interrogators using their coercive, non-torturing techniques. Hamdan was convicted of supporting terrorism but was acquitted of the more serious charge of conspiracy to murder. The prosecutors asked that he be given a life sentence. The commission sentenced him to five and a half years, but the Bush government said that Hamdan may nevertheless be held indefinitely. It seems likely that President Obama will release him at the end of his sentence.

There was something profoundly ignoble about it all. The US is a nation 'conceived in Liberty, and dedicated to the proposition that all men are created equal'.[7] Its Constitution carries the scars of the Stuart rule: 'The privilege of the writ of habeas corpus shall not be suspended, unless when in cases of rebellion or invasion the public safety may require it. No bill of attainder or ex post facto Law shall be passed'.[8] The USA pioneered the idea of fair trials of war criminals and established the model for the Nuremberg trials. The Nuremberg Charter, issued on 8 August 1945, set out the laws and procedures by which the trials would be conducted. It stands in marked contrast to the *Manual for Military Commissions*, issued on 18 January 2007 and used at Guantanamo. The Nuremberg Charter provided for forensically fair trials; the military commission procedures do not. The defendants at the first Nuremberg trial were the most senior surviving members of the Nazi regime. Salim Ahmed Hamdan was Osama bin Laden's driver. Nuremberg might not have attained such an exalted place in the history of international justice if the only defendant had been Hitler's valet.

It seems likely that the election of President Obama will change the way America conducts itself. The Bush presidency will nevertheless stand as a sharp reminder of what can happen when a nation loses its bearings and the privilege of power is abused.

In its modern sense, privilege always bestows an advantage on the holder. Privilege will be variously envied, resented, feared or (occasionally) admired, depending on the way the privilege was gained and the way it is exercised.

Resentment and envy are most fiercely directed towards those who do not deserve the privileges they enjoy. The snotty, arrogant private-school girl who treats as hers by right what comes to her by chance; the politician who in his bearing betrays his assumption that he was born to rule—these are stereotypes we love to hate.

But it is all relative. Those who are homeless, without any fault of their own, will see the tenant of a modest flat as privileged; most Aboriginal people must surely see most white Australians as privileged; to the disabled, most of us are privileged; in the eyes of those born in many parts of the Developing World, we in Australia are all privileged.

The relationship can be regarded from two perspectives: the view from above and the view from below. Those with privilege view the matter from their own standpoint, and those without it view it from theirs. But the two views are not symmetrical. Privilege is almost always noticed by those who do not have it, while it often goes completely unnoticed by those who enjoy it. For the privileged to see the truth of their own position, they must first notice the existence of the less privileged—not only that they are less privileged, but also that they are beings of the same order, for whom the sight of privilege might be a source of torment.

At its heart, resentment of privilege springs from a deep-seated sense of justice and injustice. The wretched fate of some people, compared with the great good fortune of others, strikes us as unjust. More accurately, it strikes the unlucky as unjust, and if the privileged get what they have without merit or special effort, the injustice seems all the sharper.

Ambivalence about human rights is one of the great anomalies of life in Australia. We do, by and large, believe that human rights matter, and we are broadly egalitarian in our disposition. Nevertheless, we have managed in our short history to ignore some outrageous denials of human rights. The explanation, I think, lies in that sort of blindness that afflicts the privileged. Human rights matter, we all agree. By this we mean: 'My human rights matter; the human rights of my family and friends and neighbours matter'. But after that, we are less sure. It is hard to resist the conclusion that we care little for the human rights of people we fear or hate. From this compromised starting point, the argument generally goes that we do not need any measures to protect human rights, because human rights are safe in Australia. And, of course, that is true, at least for me, my friends, my family and my neighbours.

What then of the human rights of Aboriginal people, dispossessed of the land they occupied for millennia? They were separated from the land, although their connection to it is as the connection of child to parent. They sank, many of them, into abject misery on the fringes of white society. We took their children from them because suddenly, after 30 000 years of successful existence, we thought good parenting was beyond them. Separation of child and parent—first metaphorical and then literal. The result was untold human misery. Our response was indifference, resignation and a bit of tokenism.

It was not until 1992 that an Australian court recognised that the original inhabitants of this continent had owned it when white settlers arrived. It took Australia 204 years to recognise that, as a matter of law, this land was occupied by people whose connection to it was analogous to ownership, but much more profound and personal. Until then, it was as if ownership was meaningless unless it was signified by inky scratchings on parchment. The decision of the High Court in *Mabo* was greeted with howls of derision and angry comments about activist judges.

It was not until 2007 that an Australian court recognised at last that Aboriginal children had been taken unlawfully from their parents, and that, in taking them, the governments must have known that they were inflicting harm. Bruce Trevorrow was born to Aboriginal parents at One Mile Camp, Meningie, on the Coorong in South Australia. When he was thirteen months old, he got gastroenteritis. He was admitted to the Adelaide Children's Hospital. The records show that his gastroenteritis cleared up seven days later, and seven days after that he was given away to a white family.

The white family had a daughter who was sixteen years old at the time. She gave evidence at the trial as a woman in late middle age. She remembered the day well. Her parents wanted a second daughter. They had seen an advertisement in the newspaper offering Aboriginal babies for fostering. They went to the Adelaide Children's Hospital on a Sunday and saw a cute, curly-haired little girl. They said they would like to take her home, and she was given to them. When they got her home and changed her nappy, they discovered she was a boy. That was the transaction in which Bruce was given away.

When Bruce's mother wrote to the department asking how he was doing and when he was coming home, they replied (falsely) that he was doing well but that the doctors had said he was not well enough to come home yet. Thereafter, they actively prevented his mother from finding out where he was. At the time they wrote that letter, the department had in its files a written opinion of the Crown Solicitor saying that they did not have the power to take Aboriginal children from their parents. After Bruce was given away, the state ignored him, even though welfare legislation required fostering arrangements to be monitored regularly.

When he was three years old, he was admitted to the Children's Hospital because he was pulling his own hair out. When he was eight, he was diagnosed as anxious and depressed, and as having no sense of where he belonged. He was put on antidepressants when he was nine years old. The department made sure that Bruce did not see his mother again until he was ten years old. By that time, his father had already died. Bruce's entire life was marked by insecurity, anxiety, depression and alcoholism, and was blighted by a profound sense that he did not belong anywhere.

As a witness, Bruce was a tragic figure, especially in comparison with his brothers, who had not been removed. They were strong, resourceful men who had overcome the difficulties that were experienced by most Aboriginal people growing up in Australia in the 1950s. By contrast, Bruce appeared broken and dispirited. When asked where he belonged, he stared at his feet for a long time, started weeping and quietly answered, 'Nowhere'. After a ten-year legal battle, he won his case on 1 August 2007. He died less than a year later, on 20 June 2008, aged fifty-one.

The decision in *Trevorrow* did not provoke the hostile response that followed *Mabo*. It sparked a predictable backlash from sections of the commentariat, still dedicated to the idea that Aboriginal children were not taken; it was welcomed by some members of the public for its historic significance; it added to the impetus for a national apology, which was given in parliament on 13 February 2008. But the findings in Bruce Trevorrow's case caused little concern among the public at large. How can this be? If white babies were taken in the same manner—taken from parents who were willing and able to look after them and given to other families who were thought to offer socioeconomic advantages—we would be outraged. Imagine advertising white babies for fostering in that way: come and collect one, no paperwork, no questions asked. We would not tolerate it. Tabloid journalists would fulminate, commissions of inquiry would be called; governments would fall. But it was only Aboriginal kids, and it did not matter as much as it would have had it happened to white kids—children with whom the average Australian could empathise, children who, as fellow beings, had rights and interests, loves and fears as real as our own. The unstated vanity that 'this could never happen to me or mine' confers the privilege of selective blindness on Australia's relaxed and comfortable majority.

And there is also the recent indignity of refugees—men, women and children—incarcerated indefinitely in desert prisons, without regard for the fact that they have committed no offence. They presented no risk to the community, but we gaoled them, and we held them for as long as it took to work out that they were indeed refugees, just as they had said. We made them liable for the costs of their own detention. We charged them separately for the privilege of solitary confinement. We added GST to the detention bill. And if they were not refugees, we continued to hold them until we could remove them from Australia. On 29 July 2008, the Rudd government announced a change in the philosophy of immigration detention. The new philosophy is enlightened and decent, but it has not yet been implemented.[9]

In 2004, the *Al-Kateb* case was decided by the High Court. Ahmed Al-Kateb was a boat person who was detained while his claim for protection was considered. It was rejected. Woomera was too harsh to bear, so he chose not to prolong his agony by appealing. Instead, he asked to be removed from Australia. The Howard government argued that he could not be removed and that, being stateless, he could be held in detention for the rest of his life. If we could not remove them from Australia, we could gaol them forever. The High Court, by a majority of four to three, agreed that that is what the Commonwealth *Migration Act 1958* says, and that it is constitutionally valid with that meaning. The *Al-Kateb* case should have provoked banner headlines across the country. It should have sparked outrage in every corner of the land. Instead, it was largely ignored. Even now, four years later, most Australians have never heard of the case.

How can these things be? How can it be, in an egalitarian society, that the injustice of these things creates scarcely a ripple? How is it that it is not even noticed by newspapers and columnists? The answer, I think, is found at the threshold: most Australians do not recognise the original inhabitants, the stolen generations, the faceless asylum-seekers as people, at least not in the same sense that we are people. Their humanity is of a different order. Their disadvantage is invisible to us, although our privilege is painfully visible to them.

This is the explanation Rai Gaita points to in an essay on the *Mabo* case. He writes of white blindness to the condition of the original inhabitants of this continent:

We love, but they 'love'; we grieve, but they 'grieve'; and of course we may be dispossessed, but they are 'dispossessed'. That is why, as Justice Brennan said, racists are able 'utterly to disregard' the sufferings of their victims. If they are to see the evil they do, they must first find it intelligible that their victims had inner lives of the kind which enable the wrongs they suffer to go deep.[10]

The privileged are often blind in just that way. Perhaps this kind of blindness has a survival advantage. To see daily the disadvantage of those in relation to whom we are so privileged must be nearly unbearable—at least, if we do nothing to redress it. To recognise the equal humanity of every broken spirit among the stolen generations or to see your own child in the face of every child fretting and grieving in a detention centre would be a terrible burden. This blindness protects the privileged.

The War on Terror has exposed another facet of Australia's complex relationship with human rights. It made it necessary, we were told, to introduce special measures to make us safer. ASIO now has power to hold a person incommunicado for a week, and to force the person to answer questions. If the person does not answer satisfactorily, a five-year gaol term can be imposed. Released detainees must not tell anyone where they were during their disappearance, or they face five years' gaol. If a journalist writes about a detainee's experience, that journalist faces five years' gaol. All of this can be done to a person not suspected of any offence.

A person can be gaoled for fourteen days on a preventative detention order if an official is satisfied that the person might otherwise commit a terrorist offence. The order is made in a secret hearing, about which the subject of the order knows nothing. The order is made if the official is satisfied of the facts on the balance of probabilities. The person who is to be gaoled is only told of all this at the time of arrest, and even then the person is not allowed to know the evidence that was used against him or her.

In certain classes of legal proceeding, the attorney-general has power to issue a certificate whereby neither the other party to the proceeding nor their lawyers are given access to the documents, evidence and submissions upon which the government relies. Mr H is an Australian citizen, studying at university. His passport was cancelled because ASIO had delivered an adverse security assessment concerning Mr H. He challenged the cancellation in the Administrative Appeals Tribunal. The tribunal ordered the government to provide Mr H with all documents relevant to the matter. The government provided only some of the documents, and those it provided were heavily censored. This approach was vindicated by a certificate signed by the attorney-general, which reads as follows:

> I, Philip Maxwell Ruddock, the Attorney-General for the Commonwealth of Australia ... hereby certify ... that disclosure of the contents of

the documents ... described in the schedules hereto ... would be contrary to the public interest because the disclosure would prejudice security.

I further certify ... that evidence proposed to be adduced and submissions proposed to be made ... concerning the documents ... are of such a nature that the disclosure of the evidence or submissions would be contrary to the public interest because it would prejudice security.

As the responsible Minister ... I do not consent to a person representing the applicant being present when evidence described ... above is adduced and such submissions are made ...

The practical consequence of this was played out a few months later. Laurence Maher and I were briefed to appear for Mr H at the tribunal. The hearing ran for two days. We sat outside the hearing room with our client for most of that time, wondering what was going on inside. The decision went against Mr H. The tribunal's reasons are in two parts: open reasons and secret reasons. The open reasons acknowledge that none of the material available to Mr H would justify an adverse finding. But he is not allowed to know the evidence that condemned him.

By these measures—which are still in place under the Rudd government—basic rights are trashed and the hearing becomes a travesty of justice, no matter how hard a tribunal tries to redress the balance.[11] When the laws were passed that made these things possible, we were told that they were necessary to help protect national security. There was not much of a protest. After all, everyone agrees that national security is important. The commentators pointed out the self-evident fact that it is sometimes necessary to sacrifice our rights to some extent in order to protect the greater good. While it is a fair bet that fridge magnets were never going to be enough, there was nevertheless no debate about whether it was reasonable or necessary, or even effective, to destroy the democratic freedoms we were apparently trying to protect.

Belonging to the comfortable, complacent middle is a privilege that blinds us to the operation of laws like these. But it goes beyond mere blindness: there is a kind of mean calculation that happens somewhere deep in the primitive corners of the mind, beyond the reach of language or consciousness. The calculation below the surface is this: *my* safety has improved; *their* rights are reduced: I win.

It is easy to test the calculation. If we were serious about combating terrorism, if we really wanted to stop it before it happens, we could install closed-circuit television cameras in every room of every house across the land; we could monitor them centrally and save the whole lot to an enormous database. Plotting any crime would become a very risky business. Sure, we lose our privacy, but as they say, 'If you have nothing to hide, you have nothing to fear'. Would this modest proposal be embraced? Not likely.

In reality, most Australians will not find their rights affected by the new security provisions. If you are not a Muslim, if you are not much concerned by the struggles of the dispossessed here or in the Gaza Strip or in Sri Lanka, you will not likely be troubled by these provisions at all—unless someone makes a mistake. If that happens, you will not be able to discover the mistake that was made. You will be left shocked and confused, as those hundreds released from Guantanamo Bay must have been during their years of humiliating, damaging captivity. Only then will you notice the privilege you had, but lost.

Protecting our basic rights against populism is one of the most fundamental challenges in a democratic system. In a democracy, the majority enjoy, for the time being, a privilege that they jealously guard. When arguments are put forward for the protection of basic rights, the majority answer that their rights are sufficiently protected, or that a bill of rights is antidemocratic because it will transfer power from the democratically elected representatives to unelected, unrepresentative judges.

Now we are having a national consultation about the desirability of a federal bill of rights. The debate got off to a bad start, with opponents loudly proclaiming the evils of such a document. While they made it clear that they are against a bill of rights, they did not say what sort of bill of rights they are against.

Those who advocate a bill of rights for Australia are *not* talking about a US-style bill of rights. Some people prefer to speak of a charter of rights in order to make the distinction plain. Nevertheless, there is no magic in the name: a charter of rights and a bill of rights are the same thing. The US Bill of Rights is an early example, but it is not one to be emulated. It has almost nothing in common with modern bills of rights.

The rights protected by a modern bill of rights are, broadly speaking, the sort of rights addressed in the Universal Declaration of Human Rights, which most nations, including Australia, signed in 1948. It would be difficult to find any serious disagreement about the nature of those rights—the right to life, freedom from arbitrary detention, freedom from torture, freedom of thought and belief, equality before the law, and so on. The disagreement arises when the question of protecting those rights is discussed. This is a strange thing, given that the central ideal of the Universal Declaration was protection of human rights by the rule of law.

Despite the terms of the Universal Declaration, and although the rights it spells out are basic and self-evident, they are not protected in Australia. There is not much room for complacency. Within the scope of its legislative competence, parliament's power is unlimited. The classic example of this is that if parliament has power to make laws with respect to children, then it could validly pass a law that required all blue-eyed babies to be killed at birth. The law, although terrible, would be valid. One response to this is that a democratic system allows the government to be thrown out at the next election. This is true, but it is not much comfort to the blue-eyed babies born in the mean-time. And even this democratic corrective might not be enough: if blue-eyed people were an unpopular minority, the majority may prefer to return the government to power. At times, majoritarian rule can look like mob rule.

The question is this: should we have some mechanism that makes it more difficult for parliaments to make laws that are unjust, or that offend basic values, even if those laws are otherwise within the scope of parliament's powers? If such a mechanism is thought useful, it is likely to be called a bill of rights or charter of rights or something similar.

On 30 July 2008, Cardinal George Pell was reported as having urged the Prime

Minister to give no further considera-
tion to the adoption of a charter of rights.
Presumably a person who has taken holy
orders believes in the concept of human
rights. How odd, then, that he does not
think those rights should be protected
by law against unreasonable erosion. On
29 April 2008, Cardinal Pell gave a speech
at the Brisbane Institute, in which he
spoke against the idea of a charter of rights.
He ran the usual alarmist arguments, but
unfortunately he did not identify what
sort of charter of rights he was opposed to.
Perhaps like others among the privileged,
he thinks rights are safe in Australia and
is blind to those whose rights are not as
secure as his own.

It is no great surprise that those who are opposed to a bill of rights for Australia are *always* people who occupy positions of privilege relative to those whose rights are at risk. Protecting basic human rights by adopting a charter of rights recognises that the privilege of the democratic majority should not be unbounded, and that 'if man is not to be compelled to have recourse … to rebellion against tyranny and oppression, … human rights should be protected by the rule of law'.[12]

Privilege can attach not only to people but also to abstractions. In law, certain communications are privileged. For example, confidential communications between lawyer and client are privileged. Neither the lawyer nor the client can be compelled to disclose the contents of the communication. Neither can be forced to hand over a document recording the communication. The reason for the privilege is based on public interest: the public interest is, on balance, advanced if people are able to consult lawyers candidly.

Documents marked 'commercial-in-confidence' attract a weaker kind of protection. It is not as robust as the protection offered by legal professional privilege, but the talismanic words confer a kind of privilege that frustrates lay people and journalists as they struggle to find out what is going on beneath the surface in increasingly powerful and privileged corporations.

Professions are themselves little pockets of privilege. It is the hallmark of a profession that only members of the profession may engage in that profession's work. They guard the monopoly jealously. In truth, the work of all professions includes a great deal that cannot safely be entrusted to a person not appropriately skilled. If I need brain surgery, I will go to a brain surgeon not because of the monopoly that medical practitioners enjoy, but because I want the job done properly. If a particular activity of a profession is capable of being safely performed by a person who has not had the exhaustive training usually associated with professional qualification, then the privilege of retaining that part of the monopoly will sooner or later be seen as unsupportable. The legal profession's former monopoly on conveyancing is a recent example.

The legal profession enjoys another kind of privilege. Lawyers appearing in courts cannot be sued if they perform negligently. This so-called barrister's immunity is a distinct kind of privilege that is greatly resented by members of the public. This form of privilege is also based on public-policy considerations, but those considerations are not obvious to most people. It is resented in part because it is seen as standing in marked contrast to the position of other professions, whose members can be sued if they do their job badly. Doctors especially resent it, because their lives are often made miserable by lawsuits. But the barrister's immunity is not quite the exception it seems. It is a longstanding principle that no one can be sued for what they do or say in a court. If a case is lost because the witness lied, the losing party has no right of action against the lying witness. If the case is lost because the judge was careless or the jury were lazy or incompetent, the losing party cannot sue the judge or the jury. The public-policy reason for this is the principle that everyone in court is free to say what they will. Consistent with this, the barrister cannot be sued for what he or she says in court. It is a privilege, but one that has a principled foundation; it does not exist simply for the benefit of careless barristers.

A different kind of privilege came into focus in 2008 during the public debate about Bill Henson's photographs. The photographs were the subject of an attack by Hetty Johnston. She alleged that one of the photographs (the only one she actually saw) was child pornography and should be removed from public show. Interestingly, Hetty Johnston admitted publicly that she had never heard of Bill Henson and did not know his work. Her views about his work did not change in the slightest degree when she learnt of his status as one of Australia's most famous living artists, celebrated and collected by the world's greatest galleries. They might not even have changed had she seen more than one example of his work. That's the marvellous thing about obsessive views: they are so durable.

At the time Hetty Johnston entered the fray, the New South Wales government was taking some heat as a result of one of its former members having been convicted of paedophilia and drug offences. The Henson show was a welcome distraction. Events escalated rapidly, and police seized twenty of the images from the walls of an upmarket Sydney art gallery.

When the fog of moral panic cleared enough to make it safe to walk outdoors, the police hinted that Henson might be charged with child pornography offences. This raised fascinating questions, not only about whether Henson's work was anywhere near the territory of child pornography, but also about whether, as art, his work was entitled to a special defence. Of all the issues arising out of the Henson matter, this was the most interesting.

In New South Wales, the relevant provisions of the *Crimes Act 1900* make it an offence to create, disseminate or possess child pornography. Child pornography is defined somewhat more widely than might be supposed. It means material that depicts or describes, in a manner that would cause offence to reasonable persons, a person apparently under the age of sixteen years engaged in sexual activity, or in a sexual context, or as the victim of torture, cruelty or physical abuse (whether or not in a sexual context).[13] It is a defence to a charge of child pornography if, having regard to the circumstances in which the material concerned was produced or used, the defendant was acting for a genuine 'child protection, scientific, medical, legal, artistic or other public benefit purpose and the Defendant's conduct was reasonable for that purpose'. Thus art is privileged, along with medicine, science and so on. Victorian law has similar provisions, which likewise privilege art, medicine and science.

Art, or genuine artistic purpose, is also privileged in a number of other settings. Under the New South Wales *Anti-Discrimination Act 1977*, for example, it is an offence for a person, 'by a public act, to incite hatred or contempt' for others on the grounds of race, transsexuality or HIV/AIDS status. However, it is a defence if the act was done 'reasonably and in good faith for academic, artistic, scientific or research purposes or for other purposes in the public interest, including discussion or debate about and expositions of any act or matter'.[14] Similar exemptions exist in relation to the possession and distribution of works under the New South Wales *Classification (Publications, Films and Computer Games) Enforcement Act 1995*,[15] and in the corresponding Victorian legislation.[16]

The public debate about Bill Henson's work focused on one question: Is it art, or is it pornography? The result was self-evident: it is art, not pornography. But it was not the right question, and Bill Henson was not the right target. Work can fall within the definition of child pornography but be immune from prosecution because it is also art, since art is privileged. The interesting question at the heart of the Henson debate was why art should be privileged in this way, and in other sensitive areas such as discrimination and vilification. Put more bluntly, if words or images are pornographic, or amount to racial or religious vilification or unlawful discrimination, why should they be defensible if produced genuinely in the name of art?

The answer can be inferred from the other privileged areas of activity in the same context. Something that is otherwise within the meaning of child pornography will not involve an offence if it was made or possessed for 'child protection, scientific, medical, legal, artistic or other public benefit purpose'. Similar exemptions are made in relation to unlawful vilification and to the classification laws. By inference, the privilege is a means of protecting the public benefit implicit in domains such as science, academia or art. While I willingly embrace the idea that art brings with it a public benefit, it is a proposition that does not win universal acclaim. Not everyone agrees that art matters. But it does, and for several reasons.

First, in profoundly important ways, every work of art carries part of our shared culture. It has a value that transcends money. The destruction of the library at Byzantium in 1204 and the looting of the National Museum of Iraq in Baghdad in 2004 represent losses that no one has tried to measure in economic terms because the calculation would miss the point completely. Few people would accept that a person who buys an iconic painting could withdraw it forever from public view. No one would accept that the purchaser of a great work of art was entitled to destroy it. We all acknowledge that a work of art is more than an article of commerce.

There is another reason why art matters and deserves to be privileged. Victor Hugo said, 'Music expresses that which cannot be put into words and that which cannot remain silent'. So it is with all the arts. Human language has a vocabulary adapted to accommodate our daily needs and functions. The vocabulary of any human language maps approximately to the needs and activities of our daily lives. But few would deny that there is another dimension of human existence that transcends the mundane: call it the soul, the spirit, that part of the human frame that responds to the shimmer of the numinous. In the domain of the human spirit, other vocabularies are needed. Painting, music, poetry and sculpture are all different languages, and each gives access to areas of human experience that are not available to other sorts of language. This is why works of art are considered less meritorious—or at least, less interesting—as they become more literal and narrative. If an idea is readily expressed in words, why bother expressing it in paint or music instead? By contrast, some ideas can only be expressed in paint or music: the vocabulary of paint and music share little with the vocabulary of spoken language. I once heard someone ask an abstract expressionist to say what one of his paintings meant. He said, 'No, I can't tell you, but I will try to hum it'.

Next, art is valuable and deserves to be privileged because it plays an important role in exposing truths we might prefer not to see, or that politicians might prefer us not to see. James Thurber was a popular writer in the USA in the 1950s. While McCarthyism was doing its doleful worst,

Thurber wrote seemingly innocent stories in the style of Aesop's Fables. Thurber's *Fables for Our Time* were written with animals as their protagonists. Properly understood, the fables argue for free speech and honesty, and against deception and oppression. Thurber was deeply subversive but almost impossible to censor. After all, who could justify suppressing an innocent story about lemmings running off a cliff, or a mouse that ate too much?

On 5 February 2003, Colin Powell announced the USA's intention to invade Iraq. The announcement was made outside the entrance to the Security Council of the United Nations. He stood in front of a wall that bears a reproduction

of Picasso's *Guernica*—one of the best-
known examples of the art of dissent.
It bluntly portrays the horrors of war.
However, for Colin Powell's announcement, *Guernica* had been modestly covered over with a vast blue sheet, so that
when the world's only superpower declared war on Iraq, the tens of millions
watching on television would not be
reminded of the horrors about to be unleashed. Only a few recognised the irony:
in that simple gesture, a country born of
dissent had stifled an inconvenient but
powerful symbol of dissent. A commenta-
tor observed in the *New York Times*: 'Mr
Powell can't very well seduce the world
into bombing Iraq surrounded on camera

by shrieking and mutilated women, men, children, bulls and horses'.

However, while Picasso was airbrushed out of a moment in history, his voice was not stilled. His message remains visible for all to see. In retrospect, perhaps it would have been better if *Guernica* had not been covered up that day, if the privilege art deserves had been respected: perhaps then we would have looked for better assurances from our politicians that the storm of misery about to be unleashed was truly justified.

The power of the hidden but recognised message is clear in at least two major symphonic works that come to mind. Shostakovich's Fifth Symphony— ostensibly a work of apology to the state[17]—ends with a long slow movement, which was widely understood by its audience to be an extended, haunting reference to the wastelands of the Siberian Gulag.

Another interesting example, not well enough known, is the choral movement of Beethoven's Ninth Symphony. The text is drawn from Schiller's poem '*An die Freude*' ('To Joy'). According to a 'funny piece of 19th-century musicology',[18] Schiller originally wrote the poem as '*An die Freiheit*' ('To Freedom'). Certainly, an ode to freedom would have been dangerous and radical in Vienna in 1824. The French Revolution was still within living memory, the echoes of the Napoleonic Wars could still be heard, and the titled heads of Europe had not yet fully embraced the ideals of *liberté*, *egalité* and *fraternité*. Teachers and writers suspected of liberal views were blacklisted. To speak of freedom was dangerously unacceptable. While an ode to joy would pass the censors, an ode to freedom would certainly not.

Beethoven's liberal thinking emphatically supported the original spirit of the French Revolution, and his use of Schiller's text—the true meaning of which was widely recognised—was a characteristic act of defiance. It was also a declaration of the artist's privilege well before it became more widely recognised as a crucial element of the Romantic movement that Beethoven pioneered.

Beethoven's original intention for the Ninth Symphony was carried into execution on 25 December 1989, when Leonard Bernstein conducted a performance of it to celebrate the fall of the Berlin Wall. In that performance, *Freiheit* not *Freude* was sung. Beethoven's Ninth was also played over loudspeakers by students in Tiananmen Square during their protest against tyranny.

Not surprisingly, Beethoven was contemptuous of privilege. In 1803, he dedicated the Third Symphony to Napoleon, but when he heard that Napoleon had declared himself Emperor, he destroyed the dedication, shouting, 'The man will become a tyrant and will trample all human rights under foot. He is no more than an ordinary man!'[19] He had been on friendly terms with Prince Lichnowsky for some time and visited his castle in Silesia in 1806. There were a number of guests at the castle, including officers in Napoleon's army who had been billeted there against the Prince's wishes. Beethoven was furious—his anger at Napoleon had not abated—and he refused their request to play for them. The Prince, trying to be an obliging host, urged him to play, but he would not agree. He left the castle without telling the Prince, and wrote to him, 'Prince! what you are you owe to chance and birth. What I am, I am through myself. There has been, and will yet be thousands of princes, but there is only one Beethoven.' This disdain for the privileges of birth and position is rare even now, and was radical in 1806.

Politicians today enjoy many of the privileges that Beethoven so scorned in princes. They have power that in some cases transcends their native gifts; and while some attain their position through skill and ability, others gain it by cunning, treachery, luck or simple doggedness. Their words spoken in parliament cannot be used against them in legal proceedings of any sort, allowing them to vilify people or defame them without the inconvenience of being sued for defamation. But politicians are privileged in other, less obvious ways. Even though they are entrusted with one of the most significant jobs in the country, they are not liable if they mislead or deceive the public, whose interests they are supposed to serve. The usual response to this is that the way to discipline politicians whose standards fall below what is acceptable is to vote them out. Yet the number of dismal performers in political office suggests that the acceptable standard must be fairly low. Elections tend to be fought on a narrow range of issues and to be decided on an even narrower range. Only in a lean year will the personal honesty of a politician be a deciding factor.

Most members of the public see honesty as a core value in our society. In personal dealings, dishonesty on matters of any significance is rightly regarded as an unacceptable breach of standards. The Commonwealth *Trade Practices Act* was introduced by Lionel Murphy in 1974. Almost as an afterthought, Murphy included section 52. In its original form, it comprised just one sentence—probably the most potent sentence in the statute books. It says, 'A corporation shall not, in trade or commerce, engage in conduct that is misleading or deceptive or is likely to mislead or deceive'. In only twenty-three words—a very modest number by legislative standards—section 52 introduced a new norm of corporate behaviour. It changed the landscape of commercial dealings and quickly became the commonest cause of action in the Federal Court.

In parliament, politicians are not allowed to mislead the house. They should not be allowed to mislead the public either, given that they are the servants of the public, paid from the public purse and representing the public interest. Falsehood comes in many forms. Telling only part of the truth is a notorious way of misleading the unwary, and the method generally favoured by politicians since it is less easily exposed than a direct lie.

Courts have a great deal of experience in deciding whether a person has engaged in misleading or deceptive conduct. If a person makes a statement that is false but represents it as fact, that is misleading conduct. The difficulty arises when a person offers opinions or makes statements about the future. Opinions and predictions may turn out to be wrong, but that does not of itself mean that the speaker has engaged in misleading conduct. But if a person expresses an opinion that he or she does not in fact hold, that is misleading conduct. If a person offers a prediction for which there is no reasonable foundation, that is misleading conduct.

Most people believe politicians lie. Some politicians lie more than others. It is not a trivial problem: politicians play a vital role in our society. Why should the behaviour of politicians fall short of the standards that parliament has set for

business, and which we all set for our-
selves and each other? Every time politicians mislead us, they betray the public in
a fundamentally important way.

But honesty in politicians is important
for another reason. A politician's vision for
the future generally does not extend past
the next election. Anything at a greater dis-
tance can readily be put aside for another
time. It may turn out to be someone else's
problem. If politicians could be punished
for misleading and deceptive conduct,
they would have to confront long-term
problems much sooner.

Global warming is a recent and possi-
bly contentious example. The science concerning global warming has been tolerably

clear at least since the Intergovernmental Panel on Climate Change report of 1995. The overwhelming preponderance of scientific opinion supports the view that global warming is a real phenomenon, that it is caused largely by human activity and that if left unchecked, it will lead to catastrophic global consequences. Dissenting views tend to come from people acting at the instance of vested interests.

Politicians confronted with the scientific evidence have a few choices: they can say they believe global warming is true and that there is a problem; they can say they do not believe it is true, and that there is not a problem; or they can say that they do not know or do not care. But if the opinion they express is not an opinion they truly hold, then they mislead us. If politicians had been forced to express an honest opinion—that is an opinion they honestly hold—rather than one peddled by vested interests or lobbyists, or one that is politically convenient, we might have begun the conversation about global warming a decade ago. Enforcing honesty in politicians would help extend the policy horizon beyond the next election cycle.

Politicians should be legally liable if, in their capacity as politicians, they engage in misleading or deceptive conduct. Penalties should include fines, gaol or disqualification from office. There can be no legitimate policy reason why politicians should be allowed to mislead the people they are entrusted to lead. It is a privilege that cannot be justified.

Although we are surrounded by examples of privilege, Australians don't talk much about the privileged classes these days. The preferred word is *elite*. This is as ambiguous now as *privilege* once was. Some elites are good—sporting heroes, rock stars, famous actors and so on. Other elites are bad—the regular, predictable critics of the Howard government, for example, and people who offer opinions about uncomfortable subjects (such as those that have occupied most of this essay, for example).

In recent times, Australians have resented the latter kind of 'elite'. It is not immediately obvious why this should be so. Perhaps it is because these 'elites' prick our conscience, and disturb our complacent enjoyment of the many good things this country offers. That would explain the bilious personal attacks that have been directed, over the past decade, at anyone who suggests that the white settlement of Australia involved episodes of bad conduct and serious injustice, or at anyone who doubts the moral worth of gaoling innocent children behind razor wire. Perhaps these 'elites' are resented because they are inclined to think and willing to speak out. To do so implies a privilege. It implies the privilege of a good education and the very great privilege of access to the media. Their voices are heard, which is a valuable privilege in the marketplace of ideas and prejudices. They speak as if they have answers. That is resented by those who have different answers, or who do not like the questions.

The 'elites' are caricatured as drinking café latte and sipping chardonnay, although why the choice of drink and the manner of drinking it should be a social stain has never been explained. A book called *The Twilight of the Elites* attracted more attention than it deserved. Why the eclipse of intellectual pursuits should be celebrated is not explained. There was some comfort in the fact that another book, more entertaining and better written, called *Triumph of the Airheads*, was published shortly afterwards. It obliquely praises the idea that thinking is OK; that the privilege of rational discourse is not necessarily to be despised, especially when compared with the alternative.

The tide may have turned with the election of the Rudd government. The 2020 Summit suggested a new attitude to ideas and held out the hope that dissenting views might be greeted without rancour. The apology to the stolen generations on 13 February 2008 stood in marked contrast to the attitude of the Howard government, and it was widely applauded, even though it scratched at our national conscience.

On 29 July 2008, the Rudd government announced a radical overhaul of the immigration detention system. The announcement came as a profound relief to those who had long argued for such a change. It signalled a retreat from a policy that damaged and disfigured our national reputation. I was one among many who had spoken against indefinite mandatory detention. Taking a public position on an issue was something I had not done before; it was a strange experience and produced unexpected and uncomfortable consequences. By publicly voicing the arguments against that policy, I earned the enmity of the Howard government and the opprobrium of some of my professional colleagues. I received abusive emails beyond number, as well as death threats. I was disparaged publicly by conservative commentators as one of the 'usual suspects', one of the 'Howard haters', one of the chardonnay-sipping, latte-drinking elite, and so on. It was all quite surprising, but if the mistreatment of innocent people was the new orthodoxy, it was a privilege to be despised for opposing it.

When Senator Evans announced that the use of immigration detention was to change, I experienced a strange mix of emotions. What I felt was not triumph, not a sense of victory, but a mixture of relief and happiness coloured by a profound grief that had been held at bay for years: grief at the sight of a wretched policy inflicting pain on thousands of damaged, frightened people; grief at the obvious popularity of that policy; grief at the thought that my country could behave this way. Beyond all this, I recognised at last the real privilege of having the freedom to dissent, and the support of family and friends to withstand the forces that made that dissent painful but necessary.

My grandfather enjoyed wealth and social position on a scale I will never have—that was his privilege. He did not need to oppose any government policy; I chose to, and that has been my privilege. His privilege was comfortable; mine has not been. But if I had to choose between my grandfather's privilege and mine, I would choose mine.

Julian Burnside is a Melbourne barrister. He is the author of Word Watching: Field Notes from an Amateur Philologist *and* Watching Brief: Rights, Law and Justice.

Notes

1   The Japanese secret police.
2   English law also knew this darker form of *privi-legium*: a 'bill of attainder' was a law passed by the parliament whereby a person was declared corrupted in blood and his property forfeited. It was famously used by the houses of York and Lancaster to rid themselves of adversaries, and later by Henry VIII to deal with ministers who had become inconvenient. An attainder amounted to a kind of legal death.
3   'by special order of the King'.
4   US Constitution, art. 2, s. 2.
5   'The right of the people to be secure in their persons, houses, papers, and effects, against unreason-

able searches and seizures, shall not be violated, and no warrants shall issue, but upon probable cause, supported by Oath or affirmation, and particularly describing the place to be searched, and the persons or things to be seized.'

6 *Boumediene v. Bush*, 553 US __ (2008), argued 5 December 2007, decided 12 June 2008.

7 President Abraham Lincoln's address at Gettysburg, 19 November 1863.

8 US Constitution, art. 1, s. 9.

9 At the time of writing, in January 2009.

10 R Gaita, *A Common Humanity: Thinking about Love, Truth and Justice*, Text Publishing, Melbourne, 1999, p. 63.

11 In Mr H's case, the tribunal was acutely aware of the unfairness, and tried to minimise its consequences, but it acknowledged that there was little it could do.

12 Universal Declaration of Human Rights, preamble.

13 *Crimes Act 1900* (NSW), s. 91H.

14 *Anti-Discrimination Act 1977* (NSW), ss. 20C(2) (c), 38S(2)(c), 49ZXB(2)(c).

15 *Classification (Publications, Films and Computer Games) Enforcement Act 1995* (NSW), s. 51(4)(b).

16 See, for instance, the *Crimes Act 1958* (Vic.); *Equal Opportunity Act* 1995 (Vic.); *Classification (Publications, Films and Computer Games) Enforcement Act 1995* (Vic.), s. 3; *Racial and Religious Tolerance Act 2001* (Vic.), ss. 4(b), 11.

17 Shostakovich had been criticised for his opera *The Lady Macbeth of Mtsensk District*. He titled his Fifth Symphony *A Soviet Artist's Practical, Creative Response to Just Criticism.*

18 Leonard Bernstein described the story this way when he conducted a performance of Beethoven's Ninth Symphony in Berlin to celebrate the fall of the Berlin Wall.

19 Beethoven rubbed out the original dedication so vigorously that he rubbed a hole in the manuscript.